Terra Obscura

Poems & Hidden Maps

Mary Lou McAuley

The Other Door Press

Copyright © 2021 by Mary Lou McAuley
All rights reserved

The Other Door Press
955 Clatsop Avenue
Astoria, Oregon 97103

Cover Image: *Shively Steps* – oil on linen on panel,
        by Robert Paulmenn

Previous Poetry Collections:
    The Other Door: Poems & Glimpses
    Nine Hundred Moon Journey: Poems & Encounters

ISBN: 9780578940168

For Robert

Contents

Part 1	1
The First Map	2
Liberation	3
One Room at a Time	4
Woke Up with Someone Else's Blues	5
C.A.T. Scan?	6
The Following Sea	7
Just Listen	8
Threnody	9
Legend of Truth	10
Tradition	11
Blocked	12
Sheet Music	13
Dream Message?	14
Rumpelstiltskin Is Back	15
Shadow Light	16
Transmission	17
10th Street Stage: On the Library Steps	18
As Above So Below	19
What Does a Spider Know?	20
Where They Came From	21
Who	22
Gold Dust	23
Thirst	24
Mirror Box	25
The Gnat	26
Reflection	27
Changing Direction	28
Who Is She?	29
Lullaby for My Inner Raccoon	30
Open Mic Night	31
The Desert Motel	32
I'll Risk It	33

BORN AGAIN	34
A PRAYER FROM ME	35
WIND CHIME AT NIGHT	36
THE LIMINAL PLACE	37
WORRY	38
THE WELL	39
FERTILITY	40
WIND GUST MELANCHOLIA	41
DEATH'S LOVE	42
NAMASTE	43
WASHING WINDOWS	44
INNER CITY	45
FLOWERBED MORNING	46
THE SUNNY DAY'S SOUND EFFECTS	47
WHO DID YOU SAY SENT YOU?	48
THE WHALE, THE TURTLE AND THE BAT	49
PART II	51
TOO MUCH	52
MUSIC'S ROOM	53
SOMETIMES WE CHOOSE TOO LATE	54
UP PLUM CREEK WITHOUT A PADDLE	55
THE MANDALA OF PLACE	56
TEARS OF RA	57
ON THE ANNIVERSARY OF MY DEATH	58
A. BEE. SEES.	59
EVERY DAY	60
WHATEVER HAPPENED	61
IN THE DARKNESS	62
MEMORY OF WATER	63
SKILL SET	64
A POET'S POEM	65
HOLLOW MEMORY	66
DYING STAR	67
NOW	68

Nacre	69
D.I.C.E. Deception, Isolation, Confusion, Exhaustion	70
Right on Time	71
CNN Closeup	72
Summer Night	73
Boiling Point	74
Your Own Map	75
Icarus	76
Scheherazade	77
The Path of Bones	78
Playlist	79
New Math	80
Taillights	81
That Day	82
Art in the Park: Along the Netul Trail	84
The Sinking of the Auduwabbi	86
Raison D'Etre	88
Mist Nets	89
Beacon	90
With Gratitude	91

Part I

Let's imagine for a moment that we are tiny enough to follow a bee into the hive. Usually the first thing we would have to get used to is the darkness.
—Hilda Simon
Exploring the World of Social Insects

Be. And at the same time, know what it is not to be. The emptiness inside you allows you to vibrate in full resonance with your world. Use it for once.
—Rainer Maria Rilke
Sonnets to Orpheus, #2

The First Map

Before I was born
before I took my first breath
or opened my eyes
a map was prepared
spanning the past
reaching toward
an imagined future.
When I sucked my thumb
or bit my toes
I ingested the inked contours
the veins
the vessels
the arteries
I did not make this map;
I was a human map of
my new unknown world
quickly being overwritten by information's guild
signed and dated by someone else.

LIBERATION

I don't know about you
or how you felt when you knew everything was locked:
locked up, locked down, closed
but I had wanted to do something (what? I don't remember)
go someplace (where? I don't remember)
but knowing that I couldn't
knowing that my way was blocked
started a chain reaction in my brain giving me
readily available lists of "don'ts" and "can'ts"
so I began slowly locking rooms in my heart
feeling powerless in the presence of this invasion
then something I had read long ago
reminded me
of my true power
"every lock has the same weakness: it is only as strong
as the door"

One Room at a Time

In a room
high in a hotel
the sound of a distant siren
arrows across the sleeping city
a stranger's life now changed
still awake you hear silence return
and start thinking about rearranging the kitchen cupboards
it is the only place to start
because you know
you have to change your life
surrender what you no longer use
and because of that already faded sound
you know this must be done
yes this can be done one room at a time

Woke Up with Someone Else's Blues

Don't reach down for that suitcase yet
first line them up
look at their tags
you'll see no destination
They are just traveling
carousel to carousel
Until a hand reaches down
and hauls one away
But they always wind up back
in the circle
Around and around
Until a hand reaches down
and hauls one away
So don't reach down for that one
just walk away
Someone has packed them full
of blues and lies to get to a
new place
Don't take the trip
carrying someone else's blues

C.A.T. Scan?

I wish there was a C.A.T. scan
that could show the memory rings
in our bones
the growth rings as we
reach up and drink
the clatter of our childhood
the sun flare of a new friend
the dark storm of moving away
a scan that could reveal the
gaps as they formed
the tight years of yearning
the open years of temporary light
that could flow through our long bones
and short bones
when we discovered so much deception
then farther down into our roots
where even solid rock
could release us
blown over
uprooted
lightning struck
but there is no scan for this
no technician to interpret our life rings
Who taught us what life really is?
Why do we suddenly need to examine these rings
as our barely recognized fire
flickers, about to go out?
Perhaps a scan wouldn't help
us after all
it could never show us
the one last ring.

The Following Sea

Pushed down
a gasp and froth from water's mouth rises
trough to crest
"Come back with my breath!"
the wind rages against the shuddering hull
and the ship plunges
slashing white foam against dull paint and dripping rust.
Again the surge tries the embrace
"Come back with my life!"
hissing black to blue to white
Again the hull slides away
pushing the water's breath
deep into its own wetness
Behind the ship the sea shouts and hammers and demands
"Come back!"
But the steel-hulled ship
has moved on
slicing the ocean
bleeding white to blue to black.

Atlantic Storm, John Singer Sargent

Just Listen

Looking at squares and
triangles of paper, receipts,
ink-bleeding napkins
and notebook pages torn in half,
I sat staring while
they, almost animated,
stared back.
After an hour of this
I left the room thinking:
maybe tomorrow.
Then, I tripped on a sentence,
really tripped
waved my arms and caught my balance
Because it said . . .

Back in the room
I picked up all the papers
and realized every time I looked
at that stack
I had wanted something.
Never once considering
what they wanted
to tell me.

THRENODY

Animals will return to the earth
The skies will release all the wings
And the waters will fold and quiet all that once swam
With only one element to take us back
we will watch and cry
feel cruelly treated
deceived by the end of endlessness
Hungry and naked
Some will then remember Her
calling to the Mother seldom blessed
"We can't eat the earth or the ashes.
We can't drink the deadly rain or the thickened sea.
Help us or we will surely now die."
She will gently take us, hold us, shut our eyes
And we will begin to
feel her rocking rhythm
remember Her inhale and exhale
the cycle of Her gifts
Her creation and destruction
feel the sweep of a hot breeze
After we remember
we came from Her
at last our corpses will ignite
in a final flaming rain

LEGEND OF TRUTH

As depicted in the painting: *The Truth Coming Out of the Well,* Jean-Léon Gérôme, 1896.

According to a 19th century legend, the Truth and the Lie meet one day. The Lie says to the Truth: "It's a marvelous day today!" The Truth looks up to the skies and sighs, for the day was really beautiful. They spend a lot of time together, ultimately arriving beside a well. The Lie tells the Truth: "The water is very nice, let's take a bath together!" The Truth, once again suspicious, tests the water and discovers that it indeed is very nice. They undress and start bathing. Suddenly, the Lie comes out of the water, puts on the clothes of the Truth and runs away. The furious Truth comes out of the well and runs everywhere to find the Lie and to get her clothes back. The World, seeing the Truth naked, turns its gaze away, with contempt and rage.

The poor Truth returns to the well and disappears forever, hiding therein its shame. Since then, the Lie travels around the world, dressed as the Truth, satisfying the needs of society, because, the World, in any case, harbors no wish at all to meet the naked Truth.

TRADITION

The bullfighter's glossy, caparisoned horse
had come high-stepping and elegant into the ring.
Through its bloodline refined, strong, bred to bear the weight
  of its rider.
The crowd cheered when at the bullfighter's urging, the horse
  drew too close
to the pain-panicked bull.
What glory of a tradition that has bred
one being to trust and bear another
who has so carefully dressed it for death.

Blocked

I am spatially challenged
when I see walls
they stay there
some suggest a new design.
But what about that wall,
that slope,
that impossible plunge?
Reminder:
I'm going hire a new architect
one I've never used before.
One that likes open spaces and
lots of light,
who knows that walls are also just space
holding space.

Sheet Music

Sidewalk waltz: foot prints in snow
Robert's and the neighbor's cat
paw prints lead, shoe soles follow
our sidewalk a dance floor
dots and slides following the sheet music of the snow

Dream Message?

"Eric? Where have you been?"
He says he's been in Alamogordo
taking care of some business
He says that the separation and divorce have been difficult
He looks older than I remembered
Older than he was when he killed himself
because of a woman he loved but never married
So, you're back,
I started to say
but the dream was over
maybe he's been back a while.

Rumpelstiltskin Is Back

There was a time when a debt could be forgiven
now it is a commodity for purchase.
Consider, maybe next it will be disease,
wait that's already been taken,
or grief,
maybe lifespan,
nope already on the betting line.
So, I'll put my money on the value
of the unborn.
Because
Rumpelstiltskin is back.

Shadow Light

Today my shadow got
ahead of me.
Really.
I was facing the sun
but my shadow stretched
out in front of me
attached to my toes.
I looked behind myself
no shadow there.
I hesitated
then
my shadow slightly turned
gestured a beckoning
so I followed.
Shadows have their own source of light.

Transmission

With clouded eyes
she chooses the stones,
pets them with a fingertip
to raise their heat,
feeling their smooth round warmth
knowing
these will match themselves.
One by one she strings them
while, fingers moving
she whispers her blessing.
One by one they fit together.
Again and again she nods
and whispers
and slowly a circle of small beads
is strung
reflecting her prayer.
With a final sigh
she sets them on her table's bright cloth
ready for the one who listens and hears
to take her praying stones out into the world.

10th Street Stage: On the Library Steps

Around music
who can stay bewildered
not the children
who grin and dance
and not those of us who
dance with them
which is really all of us
As parents twirl and dance
holding little lemonade-sticky hands
all my words want to come out under the bow and strum
I'll make my pen the fingerboard
my ink the strings
We've been waiting for the fiddle and
watch the musician raise it to her shoulder
wrist loose
chin tucked
appearing to rest when, at last
her moving knees and tapping boots
bring us all to the song
into it
through it
On the Library steps

As Above So Below

Every Fall the orb spiders in our holly tree dazzle us
with their design and display.
Our frequent misty mornings drape dew along the girders
highlighting each architect's skill.
This morning in early sunlit fog I saw a constellation between
our holly tree and rhododendron.
Five spiders at five
different branches had strung the Big Dipper.
Hanging in their webs
they had woven a perfect overlay of perspective
mysteriously matching the points of light that had shone down
throughout the starry night.
There were other designs,
great patterns of shell and wing until the dew dried
and anyone could see they were only spiders in a web.

What Does a Spider Know?

I've been given an extra Fall gift
by the orb spiders near our porch.
It seems the ones that build their
webs away from the house
exposed to rain and wind
grow larger faster
than the ones that build their webs
between the safer
confines of the porch railing.
The farther out you take your risk
the more exposure to what is possible;
that's how to feed your heart.

Where They Came From

No one quite knew where
they had come from
Only that there had been
a great darkness upon the land.
Generation after generation
they remained in the
crowded dark.
If there ever were written accounts
none remain
except for one account shared
with a passing stranger
nearly 100 generations later
This is what the traveler was told:
*"For ages, a great darkness held us.
From the outer edges of our dark world
came rumors of loud crashing, violent shaking
sounds we had never heard and
for a time we huddled and were afraid.
Those who left to search afar, never returned.
One day a terrible bright light filled the air above us.
Confused and blind we could not run.
Suddenly a violent stirring came upon us all
and we were swept from our earth.
Some perished but others
told of falling and landing upon
a new ground
the light soft
the air sweet
and they knew they had been transported
into the green corner of the Paradise of ancient prophecy."

---

*This is the true account of a colony of sow bugs found under a flower pot, carefully swept from our porch to the flowers below. Amen

Who

Standing at the sink
washing dishes
I was thinking of the owl
I heard in the middle
of the night.
Who?
I know it wasn't really saying Who?
Who-who-whowhowho?
Maybe we just want our language to match
to know what other creatures are saying,
give their mouths words we know
to be like Mowgli
so we can talk and dance and sing
with all creation.
Who indeed?

Gold Dust

Little golden bodies
captured,
caged and valued
for their song;
a song charged with the glow of the firmament.
Their voices lifted hearts
in tenements, parlors and briefly in the coal mine's sooty dark.
Abandoned in their cages
in flightless plunge to the black powder below
the bright feathers of daylight dissolve to golden dust,
the only ore that was ever worth saving.

Thirst

At daybreak
I saw an angel
kneeling at a shallow pool
not to drink
but to be seen
showing me a shared thirst.
The world pulled back,
my heart softened
siphoning blood into
a forgotten inner ear
and I waited, ancient
timeless, as if the earth was parent to my feet.
The angel then stood before me
placed a hand on my shoulder and spoke
"Beloved, you are walking too close to the path of Despair"
And my feet were set free.

MIRROR BOX

Maybe earth is a mirror box
given to us in trust
knowing we will see
the maiming and severing
of Life from Beauty and Love.
Given to us in trust knowing our molten despair
will cool into awareness
when we can still feel
within our being
that Life will forever reside
in the blest seeds, still enfolded in the downy pleats of
angels' wings.

The Gnat

As we sat reading
on the couch
a large shadow
passed over us
Did you see that
we asked each other
wondering
had a bat or bird flown in
Then I saw it
a tiny black gnat
in front of the bulb in Robert's
reading lamp
a winged speck in front of the bright light
it cast a large moving shadow
across its own time and space

REFLECTION

The reflection of my face in the window
begins to fade as the morning light
grows brighter
I'm still here
looking out the window
but the pane of glass
no longer a mirror
becomes a window once again.
What has changed?

Changing Direction

Today I am changing my direction
leaving the other passengers and their baggage
to catch a different ride go a different way
I've begun to notice the scenery here doesn't change
even the long way?
even the detour?
even the cabbie's way?
So I'm going my way now knowing I'll be lost
It is supposed to be unfamiliar
it shifts with each step
I sang in the darkness
in the cave deep inside
I sang because I loved what I could not see
I sang as a giving
I don't need to know where I am going
so I'm heading straight for that glittering barrier in front of me
I don't know what I need but I'm sure I already have it.

Who Is She?

There is so much more
animal in this woman
the nuzzling, purring
ferocious protector
languid companion
she responds to the seasons
fails to trust time
grooms herself for herself
she passes through magic and embodies myth
this feminine goddess
shape shifting from fox to bear to badger to horse
her clay likeness
now smashed and scattered
her artist creator long gone.
Don't try to repair her
Be Her!

Lullaby for my Inner Raccoon

I love my inner raccoon
the way she is dazzled by
jewelry displays and gold-threaded, gauzy scarves
the way she knows a rock will really
show off when held in the clear mountain stream.
But sometimes when I encounter a moment of the miraculous
she wants to grab it and turn it over and over
maybe even hold it under water with busy paws.
That's when I take her in my arms and find a tree
that is willing to hear a lullaby
"Let this just be
there is no thing inside it
it has its own food
and needs no washing
so rest in this shade.
I'll hold you and I
promise you something shiny after your nap."

Open Mic Night

These poets spin me
spin me with their soaring words
They spin me with
their surety and scents so strong
notebooks leaking liquid gold
when I fumble for my own
I find it fuller than when I closed it
a universe of words expanding
and spinning
me

The Desert Motel

It is a motel beside buckled black asphalt
that used to be a highway
the woman
in her plaid shirt
has tried to keep it up
in the back of the lot the pool is empty, leaf strewn,
the stairs pocked, the handrail leaning and she says
with a twang,
"The asshole fell in there,"
Eyes slide down looking at the empty hole for a confirming stain,
"My man, the asshole . . . "
She has a sloshing whiskey bottle
for company
lifts it in salute to the empty pool
pours herself a cup
but doesn't offer one to me
"You just passin' through?"

I'll Risk It

Dandelion stars drift
swaying on their way to the next galaxy
wobbling above their anchor of seed
take me along
I want to bravely say
but what if I fell over a highway?
or into a river?
where is the next galaxy?
a mile, two miles away?
am I willing to not survive or bloom?
am I willing just to say, yes, take me, I'll risk it?
today I'll be a poet star
wobbling above my anchor of words
swaying toward the next galaxy
am I willing to not survive or bloom?
I am willing to say yes, take me, I'll risk it

Born Again

When I briefly woke
the sheets were warm
I stretched
limb by limb
then quickly curled
fetal
into the next dream
and was born again

A Prayer From Me

Your eyes sting and leak.
Listen, you can't even this score.
You can't catch up and get ahead
of this strife
but, you can pause
step out of the line and listen.
Those soft lips on your forehead
are from you, that whisper is the only
voice you have.
Step out of the line.
Decrease the numbers that get in line
to kill with words and energy.
You cannot kill rage and strife
they are ghosts too strongly
and too long believed in.
Step out of the line and listen.

Wind Chime at Night

An angel's whisper is like hearing
a wind chime at night
you know it is capable of sound
but surely there should be light
so we could see its motion
as though it is light
not motion that makes it ring

The Liminal Place

In my dream I came to a turn in the road
and in front of me a bear and a tiger sat
the tiger rose and walked slowly toward me
and was suddenly confined by a cage
the bear only sat in my way
I've had this dream before
and in it I always change direction
and just start walking
this time, though
I recognized the tiger's cage
and was pretty sure I knew the bear's doorway
the tiger's cage was my fear
the bear's doorway was my own threshold.

Worry

I woke up with a start around
four this morning
I realized there was an intruder
in my brain's house!
Four in the morning is the best
sneaky time for Worry
some burglars are tip-toe quiet
but not Worry
It wants EVERYONE in the house
roused out of bed
roused out of bed
wants EVERYONE running around panicked
that "OH, NO! DO SOMETHING!" whirl . . .
Then I remembered my watchdog
believe me nothing terrifies Worry like the invisible
watchdog I have
No ripping, snarling, or ankle biting
my watchdog has a great laugh
I mean a really loud laugh
Find your own watchdog
train it and I promise you,
Worry can't stand being laughed at
your house will get marked with a grumpy face
that says beware of this watchdog

The Well

You could say I volunteered to fall into this well
but I'll admit I cheated
earlier I sneaked over and dropped a strong rope
   down into its mouth
it is a rope made of words
some written by others
some written by me
all the same words
bridged only by experience and love of wanting to speak,
and to place into a heart the right words
   just where they are needed.
So, I have my own rope and when I find all of the others
in this dark well, I'll tie mine to them and yell
"Pull us all out!"

Fertility

Leaving the forest of spells and
its mists of danger
true light curling the edges of my vision
the spell beginning to wane
the pain in the chest,
the spiking of tears
that longing so sharp
knowing this is the pain the earth is sowing into herself.
Yet greedily we dig deeper
take more
waste more
denying any other need
our hearts and souls shout
"Stop!"
But we know the crop must come
the glowing seeds of our fear
and love and passion and hate and greed
must begin to grow
she is the fertile one
the deliverer of all that we have given her
impregnated
she must and will give birth.

Wind Gust Melancholia

I remember hearing of a homesteading woman
who sank into deep melancholia
whenever strong winds blew
she would wander through her house
wringing her hands
twisting her handkerchief
praying to her God far into the stormy creaking nights
until one morning
she found her home landscape and faith changed
her God had not saved her apple trees

Death's Love

Incandescent bloom of grief
how wondrous that what breathes us
pulses us, moves us, sings within us
is always ours to know
is with us for hours or years
but then it leaves us
one moment
all one moment gone
we suffer by not noticing
every breathing, pulsing, moving, singing life
the lone insect wing on the window sill
the still sparrow on the deck
the quiet, curled form of our cat
my grief blooms giving me a stunning jolt of joy
for everything

Namaste

"Peace, Love, Harmony"
Symbols and slogans in the back window of the car
Stick figures of big people, little people, a dog and a cat
But inside the car
Ponytail swinging back and forth
Her moving arms waving me out of the way
Glossed lips mouthing:
"I'm late for yoga!"
Mentally I soften into my very own lotus position
a sort of passive resistance
trying to picture the Buddha behind the wheel
hoping for her sake
she is very, very late

Washing Windows

The window at night
does not create darkness
in day, it does not create light
we see only shades of our lives through it
I can be happy washing windows

INNER CITY

Both sides of her scalp were shaved
leaving the steel-grey, brittle-looking center,
so, they called her Razor Blade.
She was their teacher.
The strop of her confidence in them
and her amusement at their resistance
sharpened her words to a fine edge.
Aiming for veins of indifference
and arrogance
she could draw blood but not kill
slice through but not disable.
They all graduated
shorn and scabbed
and closer to whole,
forever scarred by their Razor Blade.

Flowerbed Morning

Nasturtium seeds
already forming
showing baby green in the throat of the flower
they will fall like a blown kiss
to carry reds, pale yellow, orange
and spring green
to the patient earth
and my impatient eyes next spring.
Nearby chameleon
shade-shifter
a white crab spider
a transplanted hitchhiker
from a calla lily
transfers easily to a nodding nasturtium
its whiter hue folding to a soft yellow

The Sunny Day's Sound Effects

The stuttering overlapping buzz
of lawn equipment
mowers, weed eaters and leaf blowers,
then the conversations of the newly arrived ravens
Questions?
Declarations!
The sunny day's sound effects
becomes a day-long call and response
until the cronks and the clacks,
shrieks, and whistles,
finally recede
and as evening settles in
the robins close the curtains
the ravens have the last word
and the owls lock the doors

Who Did You Say Sent You?

I was walking
with an opinion
we were holding hands
its mouth to my ear
then we had this
fight
'that's not what I meant,'
'but that's what you said,'
some say that's the trouble with opinions
you can never really know
who you're talking to

The Whale, the Turtle and the Bat

O, heart!
You probably saw it
the Orca carrying her dead infant
The only sound human voices
lamenting or was it

Everything has a voice

Then the video of the small turtle
Lodged in its nostril was one of humanity's
weapons of mass destruction
a plastic straw
others tried to remove it
the turtle opened its mouth
there was no sound
or was there

Everything has a voice

One morning I slid open our door screen
and a small brown bat fell to our deck
landing on its back
its mouth wide open
there was no sound
but my heart heard it
our hearts hear everything

Everything has a voice

Today we are walking through
the litter of hashtags, ring tones,
credit scores, thinking about
a new insult to hurl, the corpses of dead angry words
spoken and abandoned thoughtlessly uttered
piling up and stinking and our ears filling
our hearts going deaf

Everything has a voice

Part II

... abide in this
nothing holds you
nothing for you to hold
your wind is here
open your wings
now glide.

—James Dott
Another Shore, 'First Winter'

Life's mysteries remain and deepen, its answers unresolved. So you walk on through the dark because that's where the next morning is.

—Bruce Springsteen,
in the trailer for his movie
Western Stars

Too Much

I think I gave you
too much of my life
you seemed so much bigger
more important.
I think I gave you
too much time
too much credit
and treasure
and sorrow
and
shame.
I think I gave you nearly
all of my life
when an amused glance would have been enough.
I think I believed too long in the cities you showed me
the cities you said were mine
seeing endless avenues of glass
but only seeing my reflection
in your stolen windows.

Music's Room

Tinny chords echoing
piano keys
hesitantly struck
then pounded into place.
Old linoleum
permanently scuffed
stubbornly buffed
bounces the sharps and flats
of each struck key.
The notes want to get out of this classroom
they remember what they should sound like.
The curled edges of each page
show the composer is Frederic Chopin.
But the notes will never leave,
the book's title is their jailor
"Marches of Frederic Chopin:
For Beginners."

Sometimes We Choose Too Late

Sometimes we choose too late
as we sense the bigger hand
the bigger intelligence
a moment of touching the divine
only to feel the
singe of endings.
Lifetimes of reaching, searching,
wandering around in this
mirrored box sparkling with wishes.
But wishes appear for only an instant
so we look but walk away
without seeing the sacred doorway
our attention could have opened.

Up Plum Creek Without a Paddle

Little House on the Prairie
storyboard of my childhood
wishing for big, old boots, pigtails and freckles
and a Ma and Pa who knew how to do everything
from finding a calf in a blizzard
to mending the broken family from a neighboring farm.
Then I was an Apache princess and had a pony
with feathers in her mane and white circles
around her eyes.
Safe wandering the windblown meadows,
seeing cavalry, heroic and clean, offering
water to the mountain men strong and brave.
All reality was fiction and Hollywood never explained
white actors painted red
white actors painted black
horses spiderwebbed with the running W
gear to make them fall broken and ruined
I was in a story of someone else's making
trying to make it my own
blindly navigating my place in a world of deception
and make-believe joy.

The Mandala of Place

Near the reservoir above town
a mandala is forming
the bare winter soil
soft
becoming pebbly
turning to clay where the watercolor-water shimmers
raindrops and breezes
tease the shape
ridges form
connect
and disappear
just before it sighs its name
Eternal.

Tears of Ra

The Egyptian god Ra
walked resplendent through the dreams of Creation
His robes of pomegranate
lapis
gold and copper
tinted the path as he walked
and colored the breath that left his nostrils
As he encountered
deeper levels of beauty
the air around his head became more radiant
his eyes began to shine with
water
he blinked
and in that moment
he shared with Creation
how alive it feels to be a tear
Creation swelled in answer
and as the tears fell to the ground
they, each, golden and holy
became honey bees.

On the Anniversary of my Death

Every day I awaken
to the day I die
It is in the calendar somewhere
Maybe tomorrow
Maybe a few years from now
but it is there
and I am strangely reassured
by this
I can tell you what I have been thinking
about all these days I didn't die
I've been thinking of all the places
I've never gone
because of war
I've been thinking of all the birds and animals
I'll never see
because they have vanished
I've been thinking about all the people
I have loved and who love me
I've been thinking more about what is here
than about what comes next
I can tell you this:
Before we open our eyes
and deliver our lungs to this world
we are listening, reaching and turning
and into our ears and hands
a map is placed
it is our fleshy landscape
it has a legend that fades into the margin
please remember
this map can and often must be changed
that's what I've been thinking about on
the anniversary of my death

A. Bee. Sees.

When you see a honeybee mining a flower
she is there because her sister
in an instant of instinct and
precise communication
calculated
by the angle of the sun
the location and distance
to that flower . . .
                          . . . and waggled her little golden bum

EVERY DAY

Every day the fine ashes of the Amazon
settle onto my eyelashes
Because we have set fire to the lungs of our planet

Every day I feel the ache of the fracked wilderness
in my muscles
Because we have ripped and crushed the sacred tender earth of
our planet

Every day, I pour filtered, sterile water
into my body's thirsty tissues
Because we have choked and strangled the collapsed veins of the
rivers of our planet

Yet every day, as she gives her ashes to me
Great Gaia
stirs my attention by
throwing rubies, sapphires and diamonds into the grasses
spreading apple blossom petals at my feet
and kissing my cheek with another's lips

So now, I am breathing differently
for Her
So now, I touch the earth gently and slowly
for Her
Every day, I taste raindrops with thanks
for Her

But also,
Every day, I know why we die

Whatever Happened

Where does everything go
when memory is gone
she spoke of a man
who did things around the house
the friendly handyman
he must have moved away
she said
he never mentioned a family
she remembered
but he never fixed the screen door latch
and that made her angry with him
until an hour later
she wondered whatever happened
to that friendly handyman
she married fifty years ago

In the Darkness

In the kernel
the food that's given
can't be given back or refused
but it can wither.
In the darkness
what fed me?
What was I to take in
that pulsed in the root
of my forming flesh?
In the darkness.

Memory of Water

The dry river bed
is still bright with the memory of water
the way a charred standing forest
will wink green when the light is just right
I can see which way the water flowed
just not how long it has been empty
how long it has waited
for my curiosity

Skill Set

I never learned how to set type
or how to throw a grenade
but each one has the same impact
both can damage
but only one can heal
so you decide
pull the pin
or pull out your pen

A Poet's Poem

I wondered out loud how to learn more about
Nietzsche's coma and the dead horse
or if I might capture the brief sound of Basho's frog
maybe I could score a movie with Whitman's Song
"No explanation necessary," Nietzsche spoke up
"The frog's moved on," Basho chuckled
Whitman just walked away whistling
Then I heard a noise behind me and turned
it was Rilke's panther.

Hollow Memory

Smoke
a sour burned spice smell
like fire draining damp leaves and cloth.
I stood there surrounded by absolute silence.
The sounds came back one by one
as if they too were cautiously approaching
this strange place.
Even the trees backed away from the
low ground near the tracks.
I knew trains hissed through here
leaning and rattling through the curves
but in this hollow there was only a held breath.
The hollow held a stained memory
the memory of everyone who had ever wandered
across those tracks or died upon them
of every bird and stirring wild thing
and the memory of that place spoke to me
the memory said: Run!

DYING STAR

The petals'
moist gears
let their opening
turn in Creation's spiral
and the nasturtium seed
falls from its dying star.

Now

More quiet time now
more listening
sensing the rhythmic
great pulsing that
has always been there
but now what was familiar
deforms and collapses
and my attention
this small filter of awareness
says to me:
walk through it
not into it
not away from it
walk through it

NACRE

It can take our lifetime,
this long
breathing
moment,
while the ventriloquist
speaks about Life
and we pursue the voice
from one experience to another,
until greeting Death we discover
that the end has always been in the beginning
and the taste of the whole
was our heart's desire

D.I.C.E. Deception, Isolation, Confusion, Exhaustion

Welcome to the Casino!
I think this time we've gambled
away our dreams of justice
saying one more hand
one more spin
one more cast
so when the next dealer called
the game we felt the odds
were with us
sure, we had played this game before
and even won a few times
one more time we were lined up
with our favorite lucky dice
ready to play against the house
drunkenly forgetting
the house always wins

RIGHT ON TIME

All of a sudden
everything is in leaf
rhododendron and azalea and lilacs in flower
all of a sudden it seems to me
but in Nature nothing is sudden
the hummingbirds and warblers and robins
all arriving at their right time
While I have been listening to the stutter
of weed eaters, the drone of mowers,
other ears have heard Her voice
the call of the season
birth and abundance flight-dance and song
So everything is right on time

CNN Closeup

There is a hate that is born
but never dies
that teaches but never learns
when we are born it comes into us
with the inhale
and stays with us
when we exhale
it sits watching with folded hands
patient in its longevity
until one day we will be given a lie
it will hold its place until we listen to it
listen to it until we hear it
whispered to us by someone
whose eyes are round
like the barrel of a gun
the iris smoke grey
the bullet close behind
saying that they have
chosen an enemy who, now
must also be our enemy

Summer Night

The doorway dark
standing together
pressed
warm against each other
just warmth
without movement
feeling the fullness
of love between us
as us
the fullness of two
as one

Boiling Point

When the gift of the heart's unease
is unwrapped
amazement returns
and a kernel of joy shivers
as when the soil's moisture feels the kick of a seed
the seed is encased
not dormant
and so our hearts beat
encased
surrounded by bone bars
and callused by dismay
or fear or anger
but the seed swells
in the stillness
between the beats
like the boiling point
just before the kettle sings

Your Own Map

Leaf, root, old bones, fresh blood
the tearing strength of swift water.
Every explorer smoothes out a map
eyes shifting to the edges looking for the hand-drawn legends.
We all remember the inner map
the rounded topography sheltering blue river veins within our
    skin.
We pass through the places of our inner landscape every day.
Those times when we look at a distant cliff face
or a sunlit glimpse of river in autumn's hazy distance.
The places where our eyes translate the images through our
    heart
instead of through our brain.
Taking roads by which we encounter our fears
and find our courage.
And finally seek vistas that roar only for us.
It can take us a lifetime or a moment to remember this map.
Your map.
Its legend marks no distances, states no travel time and there is
no "X" to mark the spot called Home.
Leave the other maps behind.
This is your journey now.
There will be dragons.

Icarus

I am standing on the edge
of the last feather
all the others torn out
or singed to powder
by my high flights toward the sun
beneath this last feather
is the plunge that will prove
my dreams are no longer green
yes, I tried to touch what I couldn't reach
yes, some will say I failed
believe what you will
but remember
I truly flew.

Scheherazade

When I was ten
lying on my stomach
in front of the record player
I plunged into her story
imagining I would be killed
if I failed to entertain the sultan
I saw the silks and colors of veils
and heard the sounds of market and music
eyes shining with the knowledge
that the storyteller in the symphony
would not die
she would tell another story and on and on through morning
    and night
now when I hear the opening phrases of her story
my older heart embraces her desire to live
seducing others with the possibility of endless story

The Path of Bones

Did I only dream that I knew the way
that the steps were to be climbed
only small gaps between them
and then up again
did I only dream I started in the right place
but here is this dream remembered
through a mist of foreboding
in a shaft of higher awareness
a place familiar
no matter where it is
when it was
it is a path to a portal
if I was a hero I would remember
the cave, the tunnel, the stair
but I'm just me
remembering but never finding
the tan stubble of the field
the audience of leaning, dark-skirted cedar trees
the flash of feeling close to something
before I knew I would want to find it now

PLAYLIST

When I wrote and listened to Debussy
every word had a pearly smooth aspect
words fitted closely together
would roll agreeably against each other
never stop each other
just roll and occasionally one would slip
from sight back into a shell

When I wrote and listened to Brahms
blood watered the landscape and vistas beyond me
hands would reach for me
grab my feet
trip me
horses, nostrils wide, would die to carry
my solitary, mourning, sodden words

But when I wrote and listened to nothing
silence finally yawned and stretched and agreed
that maybe just maybe there was some little thing
it could show me
some trinket silence felt might amuse me
so I listened less often to the sea
less often seeking sweeping landscape vistas
and came back from the silence
covered in jewels and blood

New Math

We have added many years of guilt, greed and grief
to this world
It is the violence of wanting more
the savagery of wanting to be other than
better than
believing our actions were of no consequence
we maintained a kind of fire
smoldering underground
fueled by fading accomplishments
enlarged by petty trivialities and shallow loss
so we kept wanting more
willfully waging war
in a stubborn ignorance
we uprooted planted seeds, stole wings
and turned our backs
willfully subtracting our hearts from life

Taillights

Years ago, I was driving a very storm-tossed Highway 101. Branches, and little bitty parts of trees that challenged my windshield wipers whirled around me. Truly, a very, very dark and stormy night. Without knowing it, I was closing a gap, coming up on another car traveling the same stretch of dark highway. All I could see were the tail lights of the other car leading me, to a more open stretch of road. I have no idea how many miles (or years) we traveled that way. On the outskirts of a small town it turned and was gone. But, forever in my heart will be that car that held the same speed, that took the curves and the dark in stride, so that I could follow. Maybe someone is following your tail lights. Take your time. Don't shield your lights or rush. If you aren't afraid, someone will find you and follow you.

That Day

That day doesn't want my visit today
it has been very comfortable lurking
beneath my chin
where the lump pushes tears each time
I remember what I did not do

That day I walked in with my grandmother
and knew what I was supposed to do
perfume from her sleeved hanky
lined my nose
My toes could just reach the hymnal rack
tightly held and hot and patent leather
black

Paper programs snapped and rustled
behind and around and the great door hinges
pulled at the late-comer's hands
and with the softest thud they said
no more

The organist shuffled the pages before her
and boldly fired the declaring chord
beneath the notes I heard my mother's cough
the choir filed in
here my memory goes all watery and the
Good Shepherd and The Lamb in the window
melt into rubies and emeralds and lemon drops

I am supposed to stand up now
go forward to join my mother in communion
her gesture of pride in me
but that day I cringed deeper into the wood pew
refused my grandmother's gloved hand on my back
that day
I had no courage and failed her
and my mother looked away
That Day

ART IN THE PARK: ALONG THE NETUL TRAIL

I came here to read poetry to others
walkers, strollers along this river-glimpsing trail
so I opened one of the books that wanted to come along
turned to a tagged page and . . .
an unseen bird spoke clearly to the cattails
as its voice fell in moist notes into the marsh
I glanced back at the book and took a deep breath
but what I really wanted was to hear the slow fountain
of sap in the great tree beside me
and I wanted to hear the rowing sound of the river
paddling its way over mossy stones and
stretching the reflections of cotton-ball clouds
and I wanted to hear the whispers and laughter from the
swaying beards of lichen animated above me
what words could I choose to read beside this river when
distant human voices sound harsh next to the
tumbling
sweet
notes
of the redwing's song nearby
the tall cattail grasses
like fishermen casting
wave back and forth and
the sunlight is flashing green zebra stripes while
a kingfisher flies, dipping over the river
not knowing it is flying or that someone sits on a bench
and names it, hoping to write it and then read it
second hand third hand
the heron and frogs and kingfishers and song birds
not on my pages squeezing my heart already gone
what can I read to those walkers and strollers that
pass this shady bench?

a drop of water falls from my cheek blurring the
last word I tried to write
so the walkers go through and are gone
the birds pass this shady spot
the sap breathes up and down
and a tear erases all words

THE SINKING OF THE AUDUWABBI
    (after seeing Sid Deluca's collage)

By the time the First Investor was born
she had been through the Panama Canal
a dozen times.
A packet steamer carrying freight, passengers, mail.
The First Investor was born a Dreamer.
As he walked her polished deck there was
a fondness in his touch as he exhaled wistful dreams
of fresh wind and horizon.
But he outgrew dreams as currency and
turned to fondle paper and metal.
She continued her life of carrying others
just parting water going where she was told
tiring, aging, seldom repaired.
The First Investor saw her again one day
where she was moored in her own rust
and he walked the length of her once shiny deck.
Then he met a man who said the Auduwabbi
could make him lots of money
as a gift shop a restaurant in the right place
of course.
The First Investor found two more Investors
and together they bought her, hauled her
away from her familiar wet berth.
But time for Investors is measured in returns
the tight ratio of spending and profit.
So, one day, the Second and Third Investors
took the First Investor out for a drink.
"The insurance is paid up," the Second began,
"She's got to go down," the Third finished.

When the First Investor didn't say no
they rose and left.
She had never hit a reef
had never disobeyed an order of weather or men.
But when she felt the charge that shivered her skin,
felt more water than she would ever have allowed pour in
she remembered the tread and the touch
the first longing of the Dreamer
and she refused to sink.

Raison D'Etre

Dandelions
they start appearing in ones and twos
the early uninvited guests
and are quickly handed a bitter cocktail
as others arrive they are scheduled
for decapitation and dispatched into
browning piles
small girls may pick a few for a windowsill vase
but against these odds they keep and keep and keep
coming back
their job, you see
is to be the first food of bees

Mist Nets

At about three feet tall
she sees only shoes
her mother's worn tennis shoes
the border guard's dusty scuffed boots
her feet burn in her own little red shoes
how many days did you sob when you were three
how often did you raise your arms
to be lifted or comforted
only to be refused and mocked
was your play pen
cement and wire
were you ever captured by a nightmare
and held with words buzzing in your swollen heart
Mamá

Death in the desert is smelled with the tongue
and so is dust and sage and water
scorpions and snakes are seen with the ears
it is the darkness that scratches and rips the skin
alone
in the darkness
the eyes of the soul fill with blood
Mamá

Songbirds are captured by nearly invisible netting
the mist nets
the birds are gently removed
weighed
tagged
and returned to the air
the wild birds are set free
but the children
captured by steel and held in pain
keep crying in the desert
Mamá

Beacon

The First People knew with ancient shared instinct
when the salmon were coming back and
built bonfires,
beacons lighted to
guide the returning elders
to their home rivers.
For four days and nights
they let the salmon stream by
to taste again their birthplace and die.
Then with a prayer of thanks
the humans took fish from the river
their food for the coming year.
O, light me a bonfire beacon
allow my heart to stream by all who would
by their deception and greed yank me
panting and exhausted from my trust in
Life's wild and beautiful promise.

With Gratitude

To Christi Payne of Page & Book who, after moving to the other coast, was happy to continue the design and production of this third volume of poetry.

All the programmers at Coast Community Radio who kept us company in our isolation. Most grateful for all the musicians, near and far, who gave me notes that came out as words.

Our supporting and encouraging friends in the community of Astoria; famous for yummy food, super coffee, great brews, wines and spirits, but really, really full of corner-to-corner waves, shouts of "Hi!" and the best 'air hugs' on the Oregon Coast.

Greg Schuerger, Certified Beekeeper, who, by a series of very fortunate events brought us a bee box and we participated in a honeybee swarm rescue summer. One of the most holy experiences of our lives.

Tomas Tranströmer, in his poem Elegy, has a line where he says: "Friends! You drank some darkness and became visible." We have to unwrap every gift and I feel that in 2020 that gift meant we had to drink some darkness but we also became more visible.

Simone Dinnerstein, for her gift of the CD, *A Character of Quiet, Schubert/Glass.*

www.ingramcontent.com/pod-product-compliance
Lightning Source LLC
Chambersburg PA
CBHW031259290426
44109CB00012B/647